THE TIME MAN

How to Make Time Work for Your Advantage

Karen. J. Phillips

All rights reserved. No part of this publication may be reproduced, distributed,or transmitted in any form or by any means, including photocopying, recording, or other electronic or mechanical methods, without the prior written permission of the publisher, except in the case of brief quotations embodied in critical reviews and certain other noncommercial uses permitted by copyright law.

Copyright©Karen.J.Phillips,2023.

Table of Contents

Short story about time management and control

Introduction

Understanding the concept of time management and its importance in today's fast-paced world.

Setting sensible goals and prioritizing responsibilities efficiently to make the maximum of your time.

Developing a day by day habitual and sticking to it to boom productivity and performance
Delegating tasks and duties to unfastened up time and reduce pressure.

Minimizing distractions and managing distractions to focus on important tasks.

Using Modern technological equipment to streamline time management and stay prepared.

Balancing work and personal life to maintain a healthy work-life balance.

Avoiding procrastination and adopting a proactive attitude to make the most of some time.

Adapting to change and managing time during instances of uncertainty and unpredictability.

Conclusion on time control and manage

Short story about time management and control

Once upon a time, there was a younger woman named Sarah. She becomes always busy, jogging from one mission to another, in no way finding the time to slow down and revel in life. She changed into continuously stressed and beaten, in no way able to hold up with the demands of her job and private lifestyles.

One day, Sarah found out that her life changed into spiraling out of manipulation and that something had to change. She began to investigate time management and control and found that via setting clear desires and prioritizing her obligations, she should take control of her time.

Sarah started through creating a day by day to-do list, prioritizing the maximum vital obligations first. She additionally set apart precise times for checking her emails and responding to messages, lowering the amount of time she spent on distractions.

With her newfound focus, Sarah discovered that she changed into able to get more accomplished in much less time, leaving her with greater time for self-care and the matters she cherished. Her strain ranges decreased, and she or he became sooner or later able to experience her lifestyles outside of labor.

As Sarah continued to hone her time management and control skills, she has become regarded for her performance and organization.

She became capable of achieving her dreams, each at work and in her non-public life, and she or he lived fortuitously ever after.

Introduction

Time management refers to the technique of making plans and organizing how much time to allocate to precise activities. It is an essential talent that enables individuals to prioritize tasks, reduce strain, boom productivity and gain their desires. Time management is the act of tracking and regulating the amount of time spent on exclusive sports. This involves putting precise cut-off dates for obligations, fending off distractions, and sticking to a schedule. By combining powerful time control with time control, people can better manage their time and gain a higher painting-lifestyle balance.

In addition to the benefits stated above, time control and manipulate additionally have the subsequent blessings:

Improved efficiency: By coping with your time efficiently, you may allocate the proper amount of time to every project, lowering the want for multitasking and permitting you to complete each undertaking to a higher general.

Better intention attainment: By placing clear goals and prioritizing responsibilities that help these dreams, you can recognize your energy on what is most vital, growing the possibilities of achievement.

Reduced pressure: By taking care of it slowly, you could avoid last-minute rushes and the pressure that comes with trying to finish a couple of obligations concurrently.

Increased creativity: When you have a structured agenda and an know-how of the quantity of time available, you could free up intellectual space to be more innovative.

However, time management and control can be tough, especially in modern speedy-paced worlds in which distractions are anywhere. To achieve success, it's critical to have a plan, be disciplined, and feature the proper gear and strategies in the region to support you. These can also include using calendars, timers, and assignment lists, as well as mastering to mention "no" to commitments that aren't important.

Understanding the concept of time management and its importance in today's fast-paced world.

Time management is the technique of organizing and making plans for the amount of time spent on unique activities. It includes setting goals, prioritizing tasks, and the usage of techniques to effectively allocate time and maximize productivity. In ultra-modern fast-paced world, time control is an increasing number of essential for numerous reasons:

Increased workload: With advances in technology and the rise of 24/7 connectivity, the demands on our time have accelerated. Effective time management facilitates people to hold up with these demands and keep away from burnout.

Competition: In the modern competitive activity marketplace, time management skills are a valuable asset. They allow people to finish obligations correctly and meet closing dates, putting them apart from their peers.

Balance: With longer working hours and a developing recognition of work-existence balance, time control allows individuals to allocate their time correctly, ensuring they have got time for both work and entertainment activities.

Improved nicely-being: By decreasing strain and growing productiveness, time control will have a fantastic effect on a character's nicely-being.

Increased recognition and concentration: By lowering distractions and specializing in one mission at a time, individuals can enhance their attention and concentration, leading to better exceptional paintings.

Better relationships: By managing their time successfully, individuals can keep away from overcommitting and decrease pressure, leading to improved relationships with buddies, circle of relatives, and coworkers.

Increased non-public increase: By setting clean desires and prioritizing obligations, people can become conscious of their private increase and self-improvement, leading to a more pleasant lifestyle.

Financial blessings: By reducing stress and growing productiveness, individuals can also enhance their economic scenario. This can also consist of earning extra cash, saving time and resources, or lowering the fees associated with bad time control.

In modern-day speedy-paced international, time management is important for success. However, it is not continually smooth to implement. To be successful, people want to be disciplined, have a plan, and use the proper gear and strategies to guide them. These can also encompass the use of calendars, timers, and assignment lists, as well as gaining knowledge of to say "no" to commitments that are not vital. By getting to know the artwork of time management, individuals can acquire their dreams, improve their nice-being, and thrive in modern day rapid-paced internationals.

In the end, time management is an essential ability in today's rapid-paced international. By the use of effective time control techniques, people can prioritize their tasks, boost productivity, and acquire a higher painting-existence balance.

Setting sensible goals and prioritizing responsibilities efficiently to make the maximum of your time.

Setting realistic goals and prioritizing obligations efficiently are key components of effective time control. Here are some steps that will help you make the maximum of your time:

Identify your desires: Take the time to reflect on consideration on what you need to achieve and write down particular, measurable goals. These desires have to be sensible and viable within a specific time-frame.

Prioritize duties: Review your desires and create a to-do listing of duties that will help you reap them. Prioritize those duties based on their level of importance and urgency.

Use the eighty/20 rule: Also known as the Pareto Principle, this rule states that 80% of your consequences come from 20% of your efforts. Focus on the obligations, a good way to have the greatest impact in your dreams and prioritize these first.

Set cut-off dates: Give yourself a cut-off date for each challenge for your to-do list. This will help you stay centered and heading in the right direction.

Avoid multitasking: Focus on one mission at a time, giving it your complete attention. Research has proven that multitasking can lessen productivity and boom pressure degrees.

Eliminate distractions: Identify the matters that distract you and dispose of them as much as viable. This may also consist of turning off notifications, final irrelevant tabs, or finding a quiet workspace.

Learn to say "no": It's vital to be realistic about what you may and cannot do. Learn to say "no" to commitments that aren't important or do not align with your desires.

Review often: Regularly overview your dreams and progress to ensure you are on course. This will assist you stay inspired and alter your priorities as needed.

Be bendy: While it is important to have a plan and persist with it, be open to adjusting your dreams and priorities as situations trade.

Delegate tasks: If you discover yourself with too many duties, remember delegating a few to others. This will unfastened up time in an effort to focus on more critical tasks.

Use gear and technology: There are many gear and technologies to be had that will help you control a while efficiently. Examples consist of calendars, timers, undertaking lists, and productiveness apps.

Take breaks: Regular breaks are essential for warding off burnout and growing productivity. Make it a positive to take short breaks during the day and a longer smash every week.

Be accountable: Hold yourself answerable for your goals and prioritize obligations. This will help you live targeted and stimulated.

By incorporating those notes into a while control habitual, you can make the most of a while, gain your dreams, and improve your typical productivity. Remember, powerful time management requires area, dedication, and non-stop improvement.

By following those steps, you could set sensible goals, prioritize your obligations successfully, and make the maximum of it slow. Remember, powerful time control is a continuous process and requires discipline, commitment, and the proper equipment and strategies to achieve success.

Developing a day by day habitual and sticking to it to boom productivity and performance

Developing a day by day recurring and sticking to it's far an important part of effective time management. A nicely-structured ordinary can help growth productivity and performance via reducing distractions and permitting you to cognizance of your maximum vital duties. Here are a few steps to help you develop a daily recurring:

Determine your most efficient time: Pay attention to while you are most efficient and time table your maximum essential obligations all through these times.

Plan your day: Decide what obligations you want to perform every day and schedule them in your calendar.

Prioritize self-care: Make certain to consist of time for self-care sports inclusive of exercising, meditation, and relaxation on your day by day.

Minimize distraction: Minimize distractions through closing useless tabs, turning off notifications, and finding a quiet workspace.

Use a timer: Use a timer to help you live focused and keep away from distractions. Start with a small quantity of time, consisting of 25 minutes, and grow it as needed.

Be flexible: While it's important to stick to your ordinary, be open to adjusting it as wished.

Review frequently: Regularly review your recurring and make adjustments as important to make sure it remains effective.

By developing an everyday habit and sticking to it, you can grow your productiveness, performance, and proper-being. Remember, powerful time control calls for subject, dedication, and the right equipment and strategies to achieve success.

Delegating tasks and duties to unfastened up time and reduce pressure.

Delegating tasks and responsibilities is a critical part of effective time management. It allows you to unfastened up time and reduce pressure by means of distributing paintings to others and focusing on your most critical tasks. Here are a few steps to help you delegate tasks successfully:

Identify duties that may be delegated: Review your to-do list and identify duties that can be delegated to others.

Choose the right character: Choose someone who is capable and straightforward to delegate the undertaking to. Consider their skills, revel in, and workload while making your decision.

Provide clear commands: Make positive to provide clear and precise commands for the undertaking being delegated. This will assist make sure that the project is finished efficiently and efficiently.

Set expectancies: Set clear expectations for the delegated task, inclusive of the cut-off date, final results, and any specific necessities.

Monitor progress: Monitor development frequently and provide aid and comments as wanted.

Evaluate consequences: Evaluate the effects of the delegated task to determine if any modifications need to be made for destiny responsibilities.

Empower your crew: Empower your team to make decisions and take ownership in their tasks. This will increase their motivation and assist them to carry out their pleasantries.

Set clear barriers: Set clean boundaries to assist guard your time and keep away from overloading yourself with too many obligations.

Provide assist: Provide guide and assets to assist your crew throughout their obligations correctly.

Offer remarks: Offer comments on your group to assist them improve their performance and expand their skills.

Manage expectancies: Manage expectancies through speaking frequently along with your group and stakeholders. This will help make certain that everyone is on the equal page and that responsibilities are completed effectively.

By incorporating those tips into your method of delegation, you could free up time and reduce strain whilst empowering your team to perform at their satisfaction. Remember, delegation isn't approximately passing off paintings, but as an alternative approximately sharing obligation and ensuring the satisfactory consequences for all of us worried.

By delegating obligations and responsibilities efficiently, you can free up time and reduce stress. Remember, delegation requires clear communication, consideration, and the potential to permit cross of control.

Minimizing distractions and managing distractions to focus on important tasks.

Minimizing distractions is a key part of powerful time control. Distractions can slow down your productivity and make it difficult to focus on essential duties. Here are a few steps to help you limit distractions and control them efficaciously:

Identify your distractions: Identify the things that normally distract you, together with notifications, emails, or social media.

Create a distraction-free surroundings: Create a distraction-free environment through final needless tabs, turning off notifications, and locating a quiet workspace.

Use gear and apps: Use gear and apps to assist block distractions and boom cognizance, which include Focus@Will or Forest.

Set goals and priorities: Set clear goals and priorities to your work, and persist with them to reduce distractions and stay centered on essential responsibilities.

Take breaks: Take breaks regularly to relax your thoughts and refocus. This will assist you keep your cognizance and avoid burnout.

Practice mindfulness: Practice mindfulness strategies, along with meditation or deep breathing, that will help you stay focused and focused inside the moment.

Use noise-canceling headphones: Use noise-canceling headphones to dam out heritage noise and assist you concentrate.

Turn off notifications: Turn off notifications for your devices, consisting of your phone or pill, that are not associated with paintings.

Set aside committed painting time: Set apart particular instances during the day to paintings without distractions.

Stay prepared: Having a clear, organized workspace allows you to focus and reduce distractions.

Communicate your wishes: Let coworkers or family contributors understand while you need recognition, which will avoid interrupting you.

By minimizing distractions and dealing with them effectively, you could improve your cognizance, increase your productivity, and make the most of your time. Remember, powerful time control requires discipline, commitment, and the proper equipment and strategies to be successful

Minimizing distractions will let you grow productivity and recognition for your work.

Using Modern technological equipment to streamline time management and stay prepared.

Technology and gear can be very helpful for streamlining time control and staying prepared. Here are a few alternatives to don't forget:

Calendar apps: Use calendar apps along with Google Calendar or Microsoft Outlook to schedule and manage appointments, time limits, and events.

To-do list apps: Use to-do list apps such as Todoist or Wunderlist to keep songs of obligations, prioritize them, and mark them as finished.

Project management equipment: Use project management equipment along with Asana or Trello to keep tune of projects and collaborate with group individuals.

Time monitoring software: Use time monitoring software programs including Toggl or Harvest to sing how a great deal of time you spend on unique duties or projects.

Email control tools: Use email management equipment together with Sanebox or Unroll.Me to type and prioritize emails, decreasing the amount of time spent on email control.

Productivity apps: Use productiveness apps together with Forest or Focus@Will to reinforce recognition and productivity with the aid of blockading distracting websites and sounds.

Automation tools: Use automation tools along with Zapier or IFTTT to automate repetitive responsibilities, liberating up time for extra important obligations.

Balancing work and personal life to maintain a healthy work-life balance.

Remember, the key's to find the equipment that works first-rate for you and your unique wishes.

Balancing work and personal life is crucial for retaining a healthful work-lifestyles stability and lowering pressure. Here are some guidelines to help you achieve a better stability:

Set barriers: Establish clean barriers among work and personal time, which includes a particular time to show off electronics and keep away from paintings-associated sports.

Prioritize self-care: Make time for sports that help you recharge and reduce stress, consisting of workout, meditation, or spending time with loved ones.

Limit painting hours: Try to restrict the quantity of hours you figure every day, and avoid working weekends or vacations unless it's necessary.

Plan amusement sports: Schedule amusement activities, along with pursuits or social activities, earlier to ensure you've got sufficient time for private hobbies.

Communicate with your enterprise: If your painting hours or obligations are overwhelming, speak with your employer about your issues and negotiate a schedule that works for both of you.

Use excursion time: Make certain to take advantage of vacation time, and plan trips or different entertainment activities to disconnect from work and recharge.

Learn to mention no: It's okay to decline work-associated requests in the event that they might intervene along with your personal lifestyles.

By balancing paintings and personal existence, you could reduce strain, boom usual happiness, and preserve a more healthy and greater fulfilling lifestyle.

Balancing work and private life is essential for preserving basic proper-being and decreasing strain. It involves setting limitations, prioritizing self-care, restricting work hours, making plans for entertainment activities, speaking together with your agency, taking vacation time, and studying to mention no to painting needs that interfere with private life. A healthy painting-lifestyle balance can cause increased happiness, reduced stress, and a more satisfying existence.

Avoiding procrastination and adopting a proactive attitude to make the most of some time.

Procrastination may be a main roadblock to attaining your dreams and making the most of it slow. Here are some suggestions for avoiding procrastination and adopting a proactive attitude:

Get Started : It may be tempting to delay starting a challenge, however getting commenced is frequently the toughest component. Just begin, and the momentum will build.

Set precise, possible goals: Break down large tasks into smaller, attainable dreams and set cut-off dates for each purpose.

Use a to-do listing: Write down all the obligations you want to complete, prioritize them, and take a look at them off as you pass.

Eliminate distractions: Find a quiet workspace and do away with any distractions, consisting of turning off notifications in your gadgets.

Practice time control: Use time management strategies, including the Pomodoro method, to live targeted and effective.

Stay stimulated: Find approaches to stay prompted, consisting of rewarding yourself after completing a task, or operating with a supportive duty accomplice.

Embrace demanding situations: Embrace challenges as possibilities for increase and learning, in place of limitations to avoid.

Focus on progress: Celebrate your development, no matter how small, and keep shifting forward closer to your dreams.

Minimize distractions: Avoid distractions inclusive of social media, e-mail, or different on-line distractions even as running.

Eliminate perfectionism: Perfectionism can be a first-rate purpose of procrastination. Accept that it is ok to make errors and that development, no longer perfection, is the aim.

Use cut-off dates in your gain: Deadlines let you focus and stay inspired. Create cut-off dates for yourself, and make sure to paste to them.

Prioritize self-care: Taking care of yourself is essential for staying focused and productive. Make time for physical hobbies, sleep, and relaxation to recharge your batteries.

Seek assistance: If you're suffering from procrastination, do not hesitate to reach out to friends, your own family, or an expert for assistance.

Break tasks into smaller, double components: Rather than feeling overwhelmed by using a massive venture, wreck it down into smaller, greater achievable components which might be easier to address.

By heading off procrastination and adopting a proactive mind-set, you could make the most of it slowly, acquire your desires, and lead a more fulfilling life.

By following these hints, you can undertake a proactive mind-set, keep away from procrastination, and make the most of some time.

Adapting to change and managing time during instances of uncertainty and unpredictability.

Here are some pointers for adapting to trade and dealing with time during unsure and unpredictable times:

Prioritize responsibilities: Focus on the most important responsibilities first and prioritize them in line with their urgency and significance.

Set sensible desires: Set practicable desires for each day and week, and modify them as wanted based on adjustments in the state of affairs.

Stay organized: Use equipment which include calendars, to-do lists, and reminders that will help you keep tune of what you want to do.

Communicate with others: Keep in contact with pals, circle of relatives, and co-workers to stay related and assist each other at some stage in hard instances.

Be bendy: Be open to new thoughts and tactics, and be willing to alter your plans because the situation changes.Be willing to modify your plans and expectations as occasions change. Being open to new approaches allows you to navigate uncertainty extra efficiently.

Seek guide: Reach out to others for help or aid whilst you need it, and don't hesitate to invite for assistance when you want it.

Create an ordinary: Having a day by day routine can provide structure and balance, which can be mainly useful throughout unpredictable instances.

Take care of yourself: Make time for self-care activities which include workout, meditation, and interests. Taking care of your physical and mental health can help you manage strain and uncertainty.

Don't hesitate to reach out to pals, your own family, or a mental health expert for aid. Talking about your worries and demanding situations will let you feel extra in control.

Remember, it is vital to be kind to yourself for the duration of these times and to offer yourself the time and area to alter to modifications as they arise.

Conclusion on time control and manage

In Conclusion, effective time management and management can assist people navigate uncertain and unpredictable times. By prioritizing responsibilities, growing a habit, staying prepared, being flexible, taking care of oneself, and seeking guidance, individuals can boost their potential to manage their time and gain a more sense of control in their lives. It's vital to take into account that everybody processes exchanges in a different way and it's ok to adjust your method as wanted. By drawing near time management and manipulation in a proactive and flexible way, individuals can increase their resilience and flexibility at some stage in difficult times.

In addition to the previous factors, it is also vital to set sensible expectancies for yourself and others. During unsure instances, workloads and responsibilities can also shift, and it's critical to apprehend that it can not be feasible to hold the identical stage of productivity as earlier than. Setting workable desires and prioritizing what is most crucial permit you to stay focused and decrease pressure.

Another key aspect of time control and management throughout unsure times is effective communication. Regular and open communique with coworkers, buddies, and circle of relatives can assist ensure everyone is on the identical page and working collectively towards not unusual dreams.

Finally, it is essential to apprehend that a few diplomas of uncertainty and unpredictability is a herbal part of life. By developing wholesome coping mechanisms and specializing in what you can manipulate, you could better manage stress and increase your common well-being.

Time control and management are vital capabilities throughout uncertain and unpredictable instances. By prioritizing, staying organized, being bendy, taking care of oneself, searching for guidance, placing sensible expectations, speaking correctly, and developing coping mechanisms, people can grow their resilience and flexibility at some point of tough times.

www.ingramcontent.com/pod-product-compliance
Lightning Source LLC
Chambersburg PA
CBHW070321220526
45465CB00013B/1996